HELLO.

If you like music, puzzles and illustration,
you've just picked up the perfect book.
The idea is simple: look at the cartoons and
work out the song and artist. If you get stuck,
the answers are at the back.

Enjoy.

THE LEGAL BIT
First published in 2013 by Six Creative
10 9 8 7 6 5 4 3 2

Six Creative
129 Comiston Drive
Edinburgh EH10 5QY

ISBN 978 0 9575437 0 6

Printed in the UK by Cambrian Printers Ltd

www.eyetoons.co.uk

EYETOONS®

♫ sing what you see ♫

1

song _____

artist _____

2

song _____

artist _____

3

song _____

artist _____

4

song _____

artist _____

5

song _____

artist _____

6

song _____

artist _____

7

song _____

artist _____

8

song _____

artist _____

9

song ————————————————

artist ————————————————

10

song _____

artist _____

11

song _____

artist _____

12

song _____

artist _____

13

song _____

artist _____

14

song _____

artist _____

15

song _____

artist _____

16

song _____

artist _____

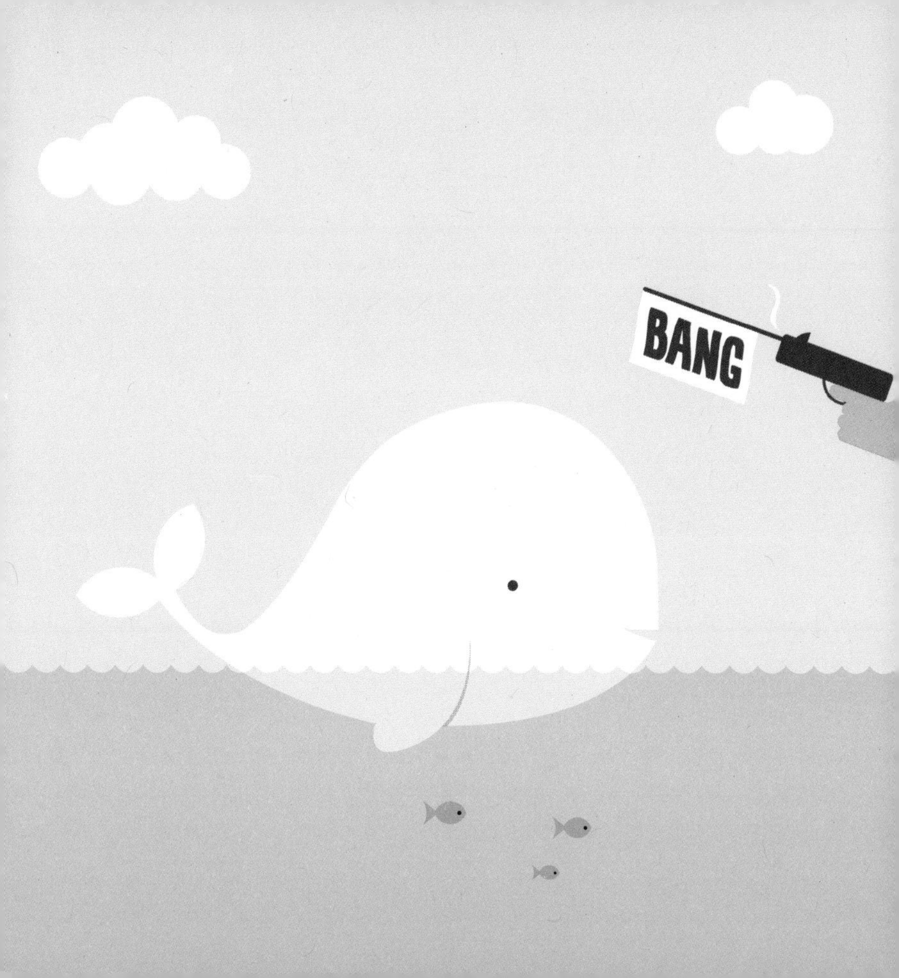
BANG

17

song _____

artist _____

18

song _____

artist _____

19

song _____

artist _____

20

song _____

artist _____

21

song _____

artist _____

22

song _____

artist _____

23

song _____

artist _____

24

song _____

artist _____

25

song _____

artist _____

26

song _____

artist _____

27

song _____

artist _____

28

song _____

artist _____

29

song _____

artist _____

30

song _____

artist _____

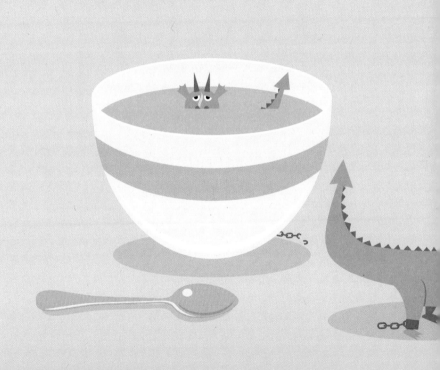

31

song ——————————————

artist ——————————————

32

song _____

artist _____

33

song _____

artist _____

34

song _____

artist _____

35

song _____

artist _____

36

song _____

artist _____

37

song _____

artist _____

38

song _____

artist _____

39

song _____

artist _____

40

song _____

artist _____

41

song _____

artist _____

42

song _____

artist _____

43

song _____

artist _____

44

song _____

artist _____

45

song _____

artist _____

46

song _____

artist _____

ANSWERS

1 ELO, Strange Magic
2 Lionel Richie, Dancing On The Ceiling
3 The Jam, Start!
4 Jamiroquai, Canned Heat
5 The Rolling Stones, Little Red Rooster
6 Bee Gees, Jive Talkin'
7 Oasis, Cigarettes & Alcohol
8 Black Eyed Peas, Where Is The Love?
9 The Police, Walking On The Moon
10 Amy Winehouse, Rehab
11 Blur, Song 2
12 Starship, We Built This City
13 Led Zeppelin, Four Sticks
14 Deacon Blue, Chocolate Girl
15 Coldplay, The Scientist
16 Moby, Go
17 Bloc Party, Helicopter
18 Toto, Africa
19 Maroon 5, Payphone
20 Red Hot Chili Peppers,
   Under The Bridge
21 Doves, Catch The Sun
22 Leftfield, Afro-Left
23 Animals, House Of The Rising Sun
24 Seal, Kiss From A Rose
25 Black Sabbath, War Pigs

26 S Club 7, Reach
27 T. Rex, Ride A White Swan
28 Garbage, Only Happy When It Rains
29 Rainbow, I Surrender
30 The Soup Dragons, I'm Free
31 Boney M, Brown Girl In The Ring
32 Arctic Monkeys, When The
   Sun Goes Down
33 Mud, Tiger Feet
34 Frankie Goes To Hollywood,
   The Power of Love
35 Gorillaz, Clint Eastwood
36 Pink Floyd, Shine On You
   Crazy Diamond
37 The Black Keys, Little Black
   Submarines
38 Steps, Tragedy
39 Meat Loaf, Bat Out Of Hell
40 The Temper Trap, Rabbit Hole
41 The Lovin' Spoonful,
   Summer In The City
42 The Kooks, Ooh La
43 Radiohead, High And Dry
44 Atomic Kitten, Whole Again
45 The Beatles, Octopus's Garden
46 The Doors, The Unknown Soldier